In memory of the hopes and dreams, pasts and futures,
lost this year in Palestine and beyond — A.A.

For Laura Coleman, who lives on her own small island,
with much love — H.C.

The publisher would like to thank every person who graciously
shared their stories to help complete this book.

MAGIC CAT
PUBLISHING

Once Upon an Island © 2026 Lucky Cat Publishing Ltd
Text © 2026 Alice Albinia
Illustrations © 2026 Helen Cann
First Published in 2026 by Magic Cat Publishing, an imprint of Lucky Cat Publishing Ltd, Unit 2 Empress Works,
24 Grove Passage, London E2 9FQ, UK
EU Authorised Representative Magic Cat Publishing, an imprint of Lucky Cat Publishing Ltd, PAKTA svetovanje
d.o.o., Stegne 33, Ljubljana, Slovenia

The right of Alice Albinia to be identified as the author of this work and Helen Cann to be identified as the illustrator
of this work has been asserted by them in accordance with the Copyright, Designs and Patents Act, 1988 (UK).

No part of this publication may be reproduced, stored in a retrieval system, or transmitted, in any form, or by any
means, electrical, mechanical, photocopying, recording or otherwise without the prior written permission of the
publisher or a licence permitting restricted copying.

A catalogue record for this book is available from the British Library.

ISBN 978-1-917044-34-9

The illustrations were created in pen, ink, watercolour and digital
Set in Bentham, Blackberry Macarons, Edith, Josefin, Palomino and Raindrop

Published by Rachel Williams and Jenny Broom
Designed by Nicola Price and Ashtyn Botterill
Edited by Rachel Williams and Helen Brown

Manufactured in China

9 8 7 6 5 4 3 2 1

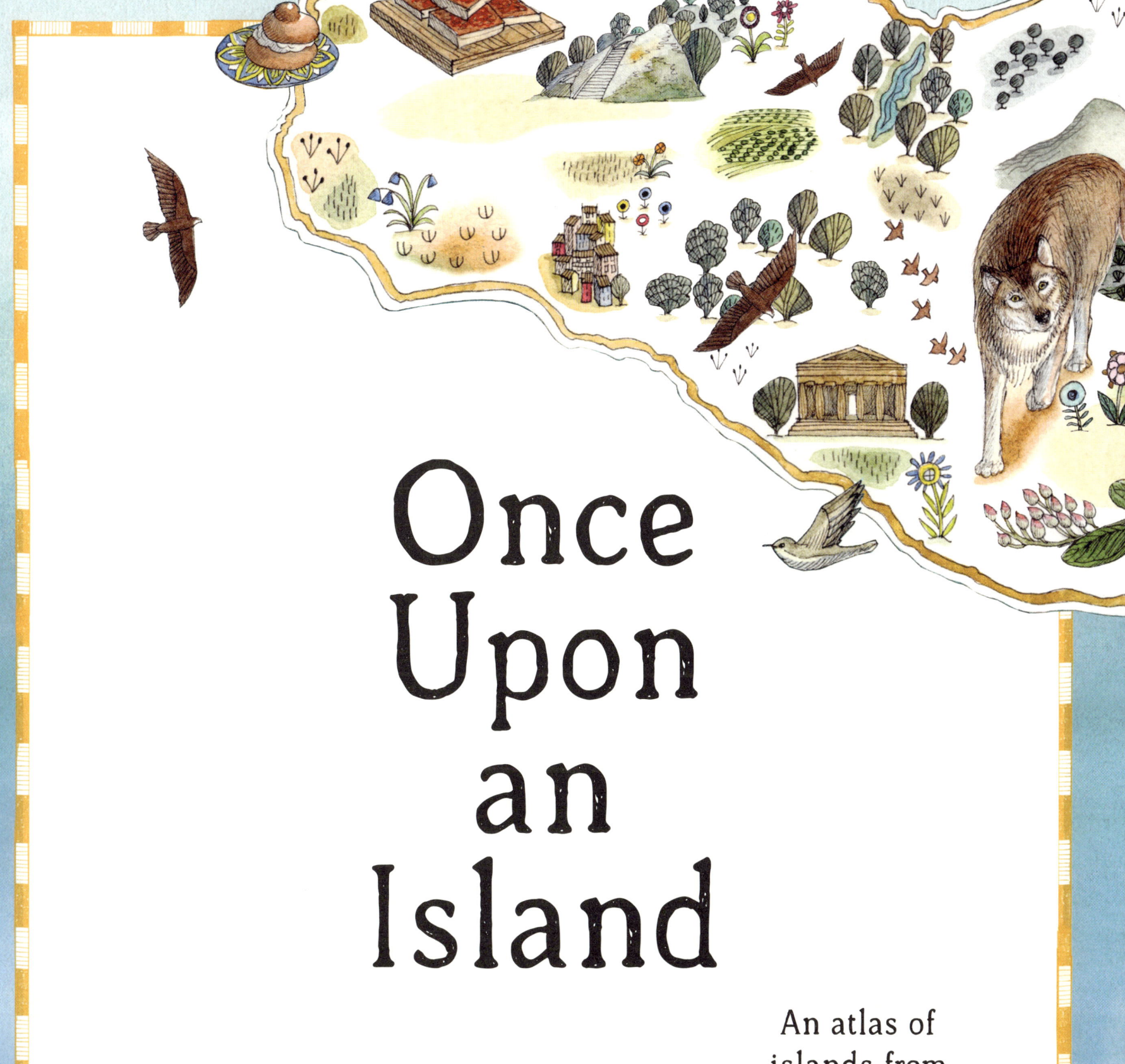

Once Upon an Island

An atlas of islands from around the world

Alice Albinia
illustrated by Helen Cann

MAGIC CAT PUBLISHING

CONTENTS

Explore 20 wondrous islands, from south to north.

ATLANTIC OCEAN

INDIAN OCEAN

SOUTHERN OCEAN

Our journey begins in Chiloé, on the Pacific coast of South America, and winds northwards through oceans, lakes and rivers to Baffin Island in the Arctic Circle.

8 Once Upon an Island	14 Chiloé	22 Samoa	30 Mumbai
10 What Is an Island?	16 Waiheke	24 Tiwi	32 Hawai'i
	18 Madagascar	26 Seychelles	34 Isla Mujeres
	20 Lake Titicaca	28 Amazon River Islands	36 Yonaguni

38 Mount Putuo
40 Sicily
42 Lesvos
44 Vis
46 Scilly
48 Texel
50 Orkney
52 Baffin
54 Once Upon My Island Home
56 Beyond the Island
58 Glossary, Index
60 Further Reading, Acknowledgements and About the Author

ONCE UPON AN ISLAND

There's a kind of magic in crossing over the water to an island.

Islands are worlds of their own, defined in their specialness by the water that encircles them. On islands we see things more clearly: the histories of rocks, plants, animals and humans, and what the passage of people, with their languages and loves, does to local ecosystems and species.

While writing about the islands in this book, I discovered that amidst the stories of struggle, these places hold onto stories about women. Stories that might disappear on the mainland cling to islands like thistledown in hair or burrs in a sheep's fleece. Across the world, islands have preserved feminist stories: from Chinese Buddhism to Incan and Mayan mythology, from Japanese and Greek history to Islamic and Christian mysticism. People have met, imagined and celebrated strong island women since the earliest stories were told — from the poet Sappho on Lesvos to Pele, the Hawaiian fire goddess.

This book, then, ends with the voices of women today, sharing their own experiences of island life.

It has been both beautiful and moving to travel the world through stories of islanders. Along the way, the incredible diversity of cultures, landscapes and ways of living shines through, reminding us of the richness that difference brings. I hope that, like me, you will find these voices — speaking of life in its many forms — inspiring: a modern chorus of hope for this fragile, precious planet we call home.

WHAT IS AN ISLAND?

AN ISLAND IS LAND SURROUNDED BY WATER.

Islands are made in different ways. Some come from volcanoes under the sea. Some are built by tiny animals called coral polyps. Others break off from other pieces of land. Rivers can also make islands by dropping mud and sand in one spot.

Some islands are tiny and INHABITED only by wildlife.

Other islands are much larger, supporting entire VILLAGES, TOWNS or CITIES.

HOW ISLANDS FORMED

Millions of years ago, Earth's supercontinents split apart, forming smaller continents and countless islands. New islands continued to appear as volcanoes erupted, glaciers carved the land and rivers and seas shifted. Later, as humans explored the planet, they created islands of their own. Some islands are formed twice-daily by tides moving up and down the land, with the gravitational pull of the Moon and Sun.

TYPES OF ISLANDS

Microcontinental islands broke off from supercontinents hundreds of millions of years ago, becoming isolated in the ocean. Examples include Madagascar and the Seychelles, once part of Gondwanaland.

Continental islands were once connected to a continent but became separated by rising seas or shifting rivers. Examples include Sicily (Italy), Texel (The Netherlands) and the Tiwi Islands (Australia).

Barrier islands are long, narrow strips of land running along coastlines. They play a crucial role in protecting the mainland from waves and storms – like Isla Mujeres (Mexico).

Oceanic islands are created by underwater volcanoes rising from the seafloor. Hawai'i (USA) and Samoa are famous examples.

Volcanic islands form when lava and other geological materials build up where tectonic plates shift. Some, like Vis (Croatia), are made largely from sedimentary rock, formed from ancient shells and sea life. Others form part of larger mountain ranges extending into the sea, like Chiloé (Chile), Lesvos (Greece), Mount Putuo (China), Yonaguni (Japan) and Waiheke (Aotearoa New Zealand).

Glacial islands were shaped by glaciers moving across the island long ago, as is the case with Orkney (Scotland). Glaciers still move and melt today, reshaping places like Baffin (Canada).

River islands form when mud, sand and rocks collect in one spot, allowing plants to grow, as in the Mariuá and Anavilhanas Archipelagos in Brazil's Rio Negro.

Lake islands can form naturally or be made by people, like the ancient crannogs in Orkney.

Coral islands are built by tiny sea creatures called coral polyps over many years, creating places like the reefs of Madagascar, the Seychelles and Samoa.

Human-made islands also exist. The Uros islands in Lake Titicaca (Peru/Bolivia) are woven from reeds. By contrast, Mumbai (India) was once a cluster of islands reclaimed by humans into a single landmass.

Lastly, some tidal islands connect to the mainland at low tide and become surrounded by water when the tide rises, like Gugh, which is connected to St Agnes, Isles of Scilly (England).

NAMES OF ISLANDS

Archipelago: A group of islands close together, such as *Chiloé, Samoa, Hawai'i, the Mariuá and Anavilhanas River Archipelagos in the Rio Negro, Scilly* and *Orkney.*

Atoll: A ring of coral islands with a calm lagoon (pool of water) in the middle, such as *Aldabra in the Seychelles.*

Islet: A tiny island, sometimes just a rock sticking out of the water.

FLORA AND FAUNA OF ISLANDS

Islands are unique ecosystems, home to incredible animals and plants often found nowhere else on Earth. These species are called ENDEMIC. Because islands are isolated from the mainland, the animals and plants that live there have evolved in their own special ways. However, this has also made them vulnerable to changes in their island environment and the global climate.

Islands often have unique BIODIVERSITY due to their isolation from the mainland.

SCARCITY OF RESOURCES often results in animals and plants evolving highly specialized diets and behaviours.

ISLANDS AND THEIR PEOPLE

People have chosen to live on islands since they first started migrating out of Africa thousands of years ago. Many of these islands are still home to Indigenous communities whose ancestors sailed vast oceans, settled on remote lands and developed deep connections to their environments. The story of how the world's most distant islands were discovered, navigated and cared for is one of the most fascinating, and sometimes difficult, chapters in human history. Island communities, whether inhabited by indigenous people or subsequent settlers, often develop unique traditions and ways of life, shaped by their landscapes, surrounding seas and ancestral knowledge. This leads to distinctive foods, languages, crafts, customs, spiritual beliefs and festivals found nowhere else.

Islands served as stepping stones for early human navigation, helping people MIGRATE by boat over vast expanses of ocean from one continent to another.

Throughout history, people have sometimes established their own republics (MICRONATIONS) on islands.

ISLANDS AND CLIMATE CHANGE

Islands are in danger because of climate change. Rising sea levels, caused by melting ice at the Earth's poles and shifting weather patterns, mean that storms and high temperatures are becoming more frequent and unpredictable. Some small islands may even disappear beneath the waves, making it difficult for people, animals and plants to live there safely. The warming climate is also affecting the daily lives of countless creatures — from corals and birds to humans.

Climate change can hurt ISLAND ECONOMIES because rising seas and stronger storms can damage farmland, beaches and buildings – making it harder for people to earn money from fishing, farming and tourism.

CHILOÉ

CHILE

AN ENCHANTED ISLAND

Chiloé floats in the misty waters off southern Chile's Pacific coast. Isla Grande is the largest island in an archipelago that stretches along the coastal mountain range where the ocean meets dense forests and rolling green hills. With its ever-changing weather — one moment bathed in sunlight, the next wrapped in fog — Chiloé feels like an enchanted island.

For centuries, Chilotes - the island's people - have told stories of magical beings that shape their world. Fisherfolk watch for La Pincoya, a mermaid-like goddess who dances upon the waves, blessing the sea with fish - or taking them away. Some say the *Caleuche*, a ghostly ship, appears in the fog, collecting the souls of the dead.

Before the Spanish conquest, many Indigenous people lived here, fishing and farming. Some, such as the nomadic Chonos, became extinct, but the Huilliche, the Mapuche people of the south, still survive, many having fought colonialism for centuries. The island was originally called New Galicia by Spanish conquerors, but the name never stuck. It remained Chiloé, meaning 'place of brown-hooded gulls', named after the birds - *Chelle* in the Indigenous language Willichedungun - that soar over its shores.

Magellanic penguin
This South American bird is typically monogamous, returning to the same partner year after year.

Humboldt penguins
These penguins make unique honking sounds to locate each other in large colonies.

Fishing boats
A large community of fisherfolk haul in the catch of the day.

Chilean dolphins
Found only off the coast of Chile, these marine mammals (known as 'tonina') use a zigzag swimming motion to herd fish.

ISLA GRANDE DE CHILOÉ IS THE LARGEST ISLAND IN THE **CHILOÉ ARCHIPELAGO**, A GROUP OF MORE THAN **30 ISLANDS** OFF THE PACIFIC COAST OF SOUTH AMERICA.

CAPITAL
CASTRO

LANGUAGES
MAPUDUNGUN, SPANISH, WILLICHEDUNGUN

POPULATION
~168,185

Curanto
Traditional method of baking meat, seafood and potato dishes underground in nalca leaves.

La Pincoya
A mermaid-like goddess who gifts the sea with fish.

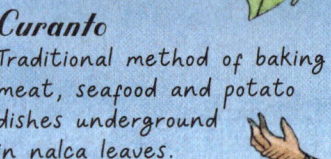

WAIHEKE
AOTEAROA NEW ZEALAND
THE LONG SHELTERING ISLAND

Far out in the sparkling blue waters of the Hauraki Gulf lies Waiheke, known as Te Motu Ārai Roa, 'the long sheltering island'. Warm and welcoming, with golden summers and mild winters, the island's rains nourish the bush and feed the streams that weave through its hills.

SOUTH PACIFIC OCEAN

Kauri
This native coniferous tree grows to a massive 50 metres!

Te Ara Hura
A 100-kilometre trail that winds around the edge of the island.

Oneroa Beach
Waiheke has many beautiful swimming spots and this long sandy beach is one of them.

Blowhole
Thrill-seekers jump from 20-metres-high sea cliffs into this blowhole, which fills with water at high tide.

Kapa haka
Children are taught Māori culture, including this ceremonial group dance.

Grey-faced petrel
Soaring across the Hauraki Gulf, the ōi bird makes high-pitched flight calls.

Piritahi Marae
This whare whakairo (meeting house), with carvings and tukutuku panels, is a sacred space supporting Tangata Māori in their well-being.

Native Bird Rescue
A small centre run by volunteers.

WAIHEKE ISLAND IS IN THE **HAURAKI GULF**, ABOUT 20 KILOMETRES FROM AUCKLAND, AOTEAROA NEW ZEALAND.

LARGEST SETTLEMENT
ONEROA

LANGUAGES
ENGLISH, TE REO, MĀORI

POPULATION
~9,420

Kororā
Native to Aotearoa New Zealand, this little blue penguin is the smallest species in the world.

Polynesian sailors began their journeys 4,000 years ago, travelling south through the Philippines, Samoa and Hawai'i before reaching Aotearoa New Zealand around 1300 CE — one of the last places on Earth to be settled.

Ostend Market
Central to Waiheke life, this market is a place for locals to catch up every Saturday morning at stalls selling island food and crafts.

MADAGASCAR
AFRICA
A BIODIVERSITY HOTSPOT

Millions of years ago, Madagascar broke away from the African continent, becoming a rare place where flora and fauna evolved without humans. A verdant, forested island, it floats like a giant green jewel in the Indian Ocean, home to life found nowhere else on Earth.

Because humans didn't arrive here until 500 CE, this island is a biodiversity hotspot. Towering baobab trees stretch to the sky, while lemurs leap through the treetops. Delicate butterflies flutter in the forests, spider tortoises crawl across dry lands and the mysterious fossa prowls in search of food.

The first settlers arrived here from Indonesia, travelling 7,000 kilometres across the ocean. Malagasy society was matrilineal, and female rulers were not uncommon. In the 1800s, Queen Ranavalona I fiercely defended Madagascar against British and French attempts to take over the island, ensuring that island rites and customs were preserved. During the reign of her descendant Ranavalona III - the third and last queen - France eventually took control. But the Malagasy people continued to resist, ultimately reclaiming their independence in 1960.

Today, Madagascar's tropical climate and rainy seasons keep its remaining forests lush, but the island continues to face serious illegal deforestation, often driven by the cultivation of rice and coffee crops.

Vary and laoka
Rice (vary) is served with a side dish (laoka). One popular side dish is ravitoto, which is stewed pork with shredded manioc leaves.

Coelacanth
Once thought to be extinct, this white-spotted deep-sea fish is found off the coast of Madagascar.

Pygmy blue whale
A smaller subspecies of blue whale found in the waters around Madagascar.

Masonjoany
The wood of the Madagascar sandalwood tree is ground into a paste and used as sun cream, a cosmetic and in rituals.

Butterflies
There are about 800 different species of butterflies on Madagascar!

LAKE TITICACA IS A **FRESHWATER LAKE** LOCATED IN THE ANDES MOUNTAINS, ON THE BORDER BETWEEN PERU AND BOLIVIA.

MAIN LAKESIDE CITIES
PUNO (PERU)
COPACABANA (BOLIVIA)

LANGUAGES
AYMARA, SPANISH, QUECHUA
(URU AND PUQUINA ARE STUDIED BUT NOT SPOKEN)

POPULATION
~14,000

Bolivian vizcacha
This golden rabbit-like rodent roams these shores.

Titicaca water frog
Considered to be the largest aquatic frog in the world!

Titicaca grebe
Found in the grasslands of the Titicaca Nature Reserve.

Trout
These invasive freshwater fish were introduced to the lake by the US government in the 1930s.

SUASI

SOTO

ISLA AMANTANI
An island home to two sacred mountain peaks: Pachatata (father earth) and Pachamama (mother earth).

ISLA TAQUILE
An island famous for its handwoven textiles.

Celestial bodies
The Incas believed that the lake was the birthplace of the Sun, Moon and stars.

UROS

Floating homes
Some 1,300 people live on Uros's floating islands.

SS Yavari
An iron steamship built on the River Thames in London in 1861 for use on the lake by the Peruvian Navy.

★ Puno
Puno
Known as the 'Folk Capital of Peru' because of its many dances and festivals.

Puna ibis
This long-billed, black-feathered wading bird lives on the lake.

LAKE TITICACA

PERU AND BOLIVIA

THE BIRTHPLACE OF THE INCAS

High in the Andes mountains, where the air is thin and the clouds drift close to the water, lies Lake Titicaca – the largest freshwater lake in South America. Fed by rainfall and more than 25 rivers, its deep blue waters are a lifeline for the people, plants and animals that call its islands home.

Festival of the Virgen de La Candelaria
A February festival in both countries, mixing Catholic beliefs about the Virgin Mary with pre-colonial Andean traditions.

Coca leaves
Altitude sickness can be treated by chewing coca leaves.

Sopa de quinua
This superfood soup of quinoa, potatoes and llama meat nourished pre-Inca civilizations.

Fountain of Youth
A mythical spring that is said to restore the youth of anyone who enters its waters.

ISLA DE LA LUNA

Copacabana
A colourful hillside town on the Bolivian side of Lake Titicaca.

ISLA DEL SOL

BOLIVIA

PERU

Flamingos
Both Chilean and Andean flamingos share breeding grounds here.

Llamas
Pronounced 'yamas', these pack animals transported goods during the Inca Empire and before, as they do today.

Frito de ispe
A local delicacy of fried whitebait, which can be fished from the lake.

Vicuña camelids
A relative of llamas, they have long and soft fur.

Tiwanaku
Around 800 CE, this ancient Aymaran pre-Inca city was home to up to 20,000 people.

For the Inca people, this was a sacred place. They believed that Manco Cápac and Mama Ocllo, children of the Sun god Inti and Moon goddess Mama Quilla, emerged from Isla del Sol to bring knowledge and order to the world. From them, the mighty Inca Empire began. Pachamama, their grandmother and the World Goddess, is still honoured today.

Yet the human story is older still. Beneath the lake's waters lie the ruins of ancient temples and evidence of settlements dating back 10,000 years. The Uros people continue to live on floating islands made of totora reeds, just as their ancestors once did to escape the Incas. The lake itself is even more ancient - possibly 3 million years old. Lake Titicaca remains one of South America's most sacred and storied places.

Lake Titicaca is the **highest navigable lake** in the world, sitting at an altitude of over 3,800 metres above sea level. Today, boats sail between Peru and Bolivia, just as they have for centuries.

Moso's Footprint
According to legend, this is where the giant god Moso stepped with his right foot while crossing the Pacific from Sava'i.

La'auolola Lava Tube Caves
Believed to be Samoa's largest, these impressive caves were formed from volcanic lava.

The 'Ie tōga
A precious ceremonial mat, woven from lau'ie (pandanus) leaves.

Mount Matavanu
An active volcano!

Tooth-billed pigeon
The rainforest-dwelling manumea is Samoa's national bird and found nowhere else in the world.

A'opo Conservation Area
A nature reserve, home to lush rainforests.

Etak
An ancient Polynesian navigation technique in which the sailor visualizes the canoe as stationary while the islands appear to move past, guiding the way to the destination.

Alofaaga Blowholes
Spectacular natural blowholes line this volcanic coastline.

Salelologa Market
Traditional handicrafts are sold here, including jewellery made from coconuts.

SAMOA

OCEANIA

THE HEARTBEAT OF POLYNESIA

Rising out of the South Pacific Ocean, Samoa is a microstate of volcanic peaks, rainforests and cloud-draped valleys at the heart of Polynesia.

Around 3,000 years ago, the Lapita people, originating from New Guinea, sailed eastward in canoes. These voyagers used the stars and other islands of Polynesia to navigate the vast ocean waters until they reached the shores of Samoa. This tropical island, with its cloud forests, deep valleys and beautiful beaches, became the heartbeat of the Polynesian civilization.

Once entirely blanketed by forest, Samoa has seen thousands of years of human settlement reshape its landscape. However, in recent years huge efforts have been made to preserve and grow indigenous forests — efforts that are also deeply tied to the island's commitment to climate justice.

Samoa also celebrates its robust resilience in the face of European colonialism. It became the first Pacific Island nation to gain independence. Samoans honour powerful female and non-binary figures, including the Fa'afafine, people who today embody both masculine and feminine traits. Among the most legendary figures in Samoan history is Nafanua, a warrior queen who rose to divine status. Today, from the rhythmic beats of its inhabitants' music to peaceful prayer ceremonies, Samoa is a place where ancient traditions thrive alongside a joyful, welcoming spirit.

SAMOA IS MADE UP OF TWO MAIN ISLANDS, **UPOLU** AND **SAVAI'I**, ALONG WITH SEVEN SMALLER ISLETS.

CAPITAL
APIA (UPOLU)

LANGUAGES
ENGLISH, SAMOAN

POPULATION
~223,000

The Samoan way of life, or **Fa'a Samoa**, places a strong emphasis on community and family. Extended families (or aiga) elect chiefs (or matai) to represent them in village councils, where decisions are made collectively. This fosters a sense of connection and happiness — so much so that there is no word for 'stress' in their language!

N
SOUTH PACIFIC OCEAN

Sa
This evening prayer curfew is observed in some villages, marked by the blowing of a conch shell.

Lavalava
A sarong worn by both men and women, perfect for Samoa's tropical weather!

Robert Louis Stevenson Museum
The final home of the Scottish author fondly known by locals as 'Tusitala', teller of tales.

Mulinu'u
A small village housing Samoa's parliament, blending traditional culture with modern governance.

Flat-billed kingfisher
A coastal bird with a strong bill capable of cracking crab shells.

Teuila
Samoa's national flower, featured on the 20 tālā banknote alongside the manumea, Samoa's national bird.

Umu
An oven made of hot volcanic rocks, with banana leaves covering the top to trap the heat.

Fuipisia Falls
A pair of jungle waterfalls.

UPOLU

O Le Pupu-Pue
The first national park in the South Pacific — and the perfect habitat for flying foxes!

Palusami
Corned beef or mutton and coconut cream wrapped in taro leaves.

Sāsā
A traditional, often seated dance performed to the rhythm of a pātē log drum.

Samoan flying fox
Samoans call this medium-sized bat pe'a. The females give birth to a single pup each year.

To Sua Ocean Trench
This 'giant swimming hole' is formed from a collapsed lava tube some 30 metres deep.

Fautasi
Traditional longboats; crews of up to 50 race every June to celebrate Samoa's independence.

Kilikiti
A bat-and-ball sport played in big teams, unique to Samoa.

Coconut crab
The largest species of crab in the world, known in Samoa as the ūū.

Kava
A ceremonial drink made from the root of a pepper plant, traditionally drunk from a wooden bowl.

TIWI
AUSTRALIA
PAINTING THE DREAMTIME

The Tiwi Islands, located in the Top End of Australia, are alive with Indigenous stories, traditions and art. These islands have been home to the Tiwi people for thousands of years, ever since they became separated from the mainland at the end of the last Ice Age. Over time, the Tiwi developed their own language, customs and way of life.

One of the most magical Tiwi stories tells of Mudungkala, a blind woman who travelled across the islands with her three children during the Dreaming. As she walked, fresh water bubbled up behind her, shaping the islands' lush rainforests, beaches and mangroves.

Unlike many other cultures, Tiwi islanders trace their family lines through their mothers, or *yiminga*, the 'line of life'. Patrilineal inheritance comes through the 'Dreaming': the passing on of sacred stories and totems.

For the Tiwi, art is a way of telling tales. Using natural pigments, they paint geometric patterns on wood, bark and their bodies. These designs share history, family connections and important events. Every year, the community comes together to celebrate their Indigenous Australian culture through dance, song and storytelling – keeping their Tiwi traditions alive.

Crested terns
The Tiwi Islands host the world's largest breeding colony of these graceful seabirds.

Munupi Arts & Crafts Association
An art centre that celebrates Tiwi culture.

BATHURST ISLAND

Tiwi Bombers Football Club
Yiloga, or Australian Rules Football, is played here.

Wallabies
Wallabies are the only macropods on the Tiwi Islands.

Patakijiyali Museum
The museum holds records about the Tiwi spirituality.

Tiwi Land Council
A community organization formed in 1978 to help the Tiwi people protect their land and sea.

Tiwi hooded robin
This small robin, last seen in 1992, may now be extinct.

Yoi
A series of dances, some totemic (inherited from the mother), and others ceremonial (from the father).

The islands' **Aussie Rules Football** team, Tiwi Bombers, was the first All-Aboriginal team to play in a major league. Aussie Rules Football mixes Gaelic football with the Indigenous game Marn Grook. Tiwi has the highest rate of participation in Australia.

Seychelles sunbirds
Known as 'kolibri' in Creole, these birds lay their eggs in a nest made of grass and spider silk.

Séga and Moutya
Two dance forms in Seychellois culture, accompanied by African drums.

Bouyon
A fish soup made with rabbitfish or red snapper.

NORTH ISLAND

SEYCHELLES IS MADE UP OF TWO MAIN ISLAND GROUPS: THE **MAHÉ GROUP** (OF MORE THAN 40 CENTRAL, MOUNTAINOUS ISLANDS) AND AN **OUTER GROUP** (OF OVER 70 FLATTER CORAL ISLANDS).

CAPITAL
VICTORIA (MAHÉ)

LANGUAGES
ENGLISH, FRENCH, KREOL SESELWA (SEYCHELLOIS CREOLE)

POPULATION
~130,000

SILHOUETTE

Tiger chameleon
This reptile with a pointy chin is found only in Seychelles' tropical forests.

Seychelles scops-owl
This elusive bird lives in Morne Seychellois National Park and is more often heard than seen.

National Botanical Garden
Home to over 280 plant species.

Trois Frères Trail
This hike features the Seychelles' only carnivorous plant, Nepenthes pervillei.

CERF

Latanier palm
A rainforest plant with black spines, which likely stopped it being overgrazed by giant tortoises.

Seychelles society is '**matrifocal**', meaning women play a central role in both the home and the community, shaping the culture with their leadership and wisdom.

Victoria

MAHÉ

Seychelles giant tortoise
Once hunted almost to extinction by European sailors, this reptile is now a protected species.

Aldabra
The world's second-largest raised coral atoll, and home to the world's largest population of giant tortoises.

Mare aux Cochons
This forest is filled with cinnamon trees, one of the Seychelles' earliest cash crops.

Jellyfish tree
The English name of this endangered species comes from the fruit's upturned jellyfish-like shape.

Screw pines
These 20-metre-tall trees are salt-resistant, allowing them to thrive by the sea.

Praslin National Park
Home to the Seychelles black parrot.

Coco de mer
A rare palm tree that produces the world's largest and heaviest seeds!

Hawksbill turtles
The Seychelles is one of three places where females lay eggs during the day.

Satini reken
A chutney of flaked shark, fried with onions and spices, topped with lime and bilimbi juice (from the cucumber tree).

Seychelles warbler
Songbird saved from extinction by conservation efforts on Cousin Island Reserve.

Fruit bats
These large bats, also known as flying foxes, soar between islands to feed on fruit.

Seychelles swiftlets
Known as 'zirondel' in Creole, these birds breed in caves on the islands of Mahé, Praslin and La Digue.

Ladob
A staple dish based on plantains, breadfruit and cassava.

Coral
Reef ecosystems are built by tiny animals called coral polyps. When stressed by climate change, coral loses its vibrant colours and turns white.

SEYCHELLES
AFRICA
HOME OF THE COCO DE MER

Lying in the warm, turquoise waters of the Indian Ocean, the Seychelles is an archipelago of over a hundred islands, dotted off the coast of Africa.

With sunny skies and gentle breezes year-round, the islands enjoy a warm, humid climate – ideal for lush vegetation and vibrant wildlife. Some of the islands are flat and coralline (resembling coral), while others rise dramatically with granite peaks, creating a varied landscape.

The Seychelles were uninhabited until the eighteenth century, when they were settled by European colonizers. Under French and later British rule, the islands became sites to grow cash crops like cotton, by bringing enslaved Africans to work the land. Large-scale deforestation occurred, but in 1976 the Seychelles gained independence from the UK, becoming a sovereign republic. Since then huge conservation efforts have been put in place. Today, 88 per cent of the Seychelles' land area is forested.

Among the islands' many natural wonders, the coco de mer stands out. This rare palm, with both male and female trees, produces giant seeds steeped in folklore and legend – which are attractive to scientists, tourists and poachers alike.

THE AMAZON, BRAZIL

Uakari
A red-faced monkey native to the region.

Parque Nacional do Jaú
A protected national park that is kept safe from people cutting down trees.

Airão Velho
A ghost town from the colonial rubber boom of the 1800s.

Fish species richness
The river is one of the richest habitats for fish, including giant catfish and arapaima.

Women from the Saracá Indigenous community along the Rio Negro are leading protests against **climate change**. Dropping river levels are threatening the land, wildlife and their way of life.

Açaí berries
These native dark purple grape-like fruits are packed with nutrients.

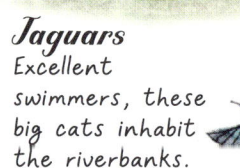
COMUNIDADE SACARÁ

Jaguars
Excellent swimmers, these big cats inhabit the riverbanks.

Terra firme forests
Moist tropical forests where Brazil nut, mahogany and rubber trees thrive.

Farofa
Toasted cassava flour, a famous Brazilian side dish.

Camu-camu
A vitamin-rich sour berry native to the rainforest.

AMAZON RIVER ISLANDS

BRAZIL

THE FLOATING FOREST

Deep in the heart of the Amazon Rainforest, where the air is thick with heat and the sound of wildlife never stops, the largest river archipelagos in the world, Mariuá and Anavilhanas, rise from the waters of the Rio Negro. Interlaced by streams, these islands are home to one of Earth's most biodiverse ecosystems.

Unlike ocean islands, river islands are surrounded by freshwater, not saltwater. Towering trees, tangled vines and hidden lagoons shelter countless creatures, including pink river dolphins, giant otters, sloths and colourful macaws. Their unique 'floating forest' ecosystems are shaped by seasonal floods.

The Amazon River flows through eight countries before reaching Brazil, where its milky-brown waters meet the Rio Negro in a swirling spectacle. The river's name, inspired by Greek myths, recalls the Indigenous women who fought Spanish colonialists in the 1500s with strength and bravery.

Indigenous women and men still live here, their sustainable practices and lifestyles helping to guide the rest of the world in how to protect the rainforest's delicate balance.

Serra do Aracá
A 1.5-billion-year-old flat-topped mountain in the northern forest.

Bird paradise
Macaws, vultures, egrets, kingfishers, herons and hummingbirds inhabit the forest.

Igapó
A Brazilian term for forests flooded by dark, swampy river waters for half the year.

Yacare caimans
These alligator relatives are native to Central and South America.

First people
Around 100 Indigenous groups live in the Amazon, many uncontacted by the outside world.

Giant otter
The world's largest otter feeds on fish in the rivers.

Teatro Amazonas
An ornate opera house built in 1896, with Glasgow steel, French tiles and Italian marble.

Manaus

Amazon River dolphins
Born grey, these dolphins turn pink with age. They have flexible necks to dodge submerged trees.

Confluence
The 'Encontro das Águas', where the Amazon River and Rio Negro meet.

THE AMAZON RIVER ISLANDS ARE LOCATED WITHIN THE **AMAZON RIVER BASIN** IN SOUTH AMERICA.

<u>CAPITAL OF AMAZONAS STATE</u>
MANAUS

<u>LANGUAGES</u>
PORTUGUESE, SPANISH, ALONG WITH 300 INDIGENOUS LANGUAGES, BELONGING TO VARIOUS LINGUISTIC FAMILIES (TUPI, ARAWAK, CARIB, MACRO-JÊ)

<u>POPULATION</u>
850 PEOPLE IN THE RIO NEGRO SUSTAINABLE DEVELOPMENT RESERVE OF WHICH 85 ARE SARACÁ

RIO NEGRO

AMAZON RIVER

MUMBAI

INDIA

THE CITY OF SEVEN ISLANDS

Long ago Mumbai wasn't one city, but seven little islands. Over the centuries these islands have been home to fishing villages and forts, Buddhist monasteries and Sufi shrines, Hindu temples, cathedrals, markets and mangroves. By 1838, when India was still under British colonial rule, engineers linked the islands together to form the heart of Mumbai as we know it today.

Now, this vibrant city is India's fashion, commercial and film capital, a place where skyscrapers rise beside old forts and ancient shrines. People from Mumbai, called Mumbaikers, love their home for its blend of old and new. All of India is here: its many languages, religions, foods and fashions. The weather is warm and humid for most of the year, with monsoon rains drenching the city in summer. On Chowpatty Beach, you can walk by the Arabian Sea and imagine the islands before they became one.

Today, Mumbai - home to around 21 million people, from low-income residents to Bollywood movie stars - is India's most populous city. As this megacity grows, the spirit of its original seven islands lives on, in its people, its history and its energetic atmosphere.

Mumbai's diversity is reflected in its **religious spaces**. The city's earliest temples likely belonged to fishing communities. Muslims, present in India since at least the eighth century as traders and later rulers, built mosques and Sufi shrines. The Portuguese and later the British constructed churches.

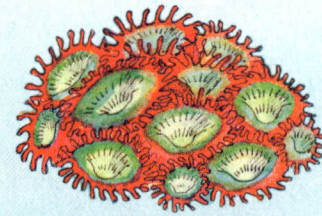

Palythoa mutuki
This soft coral glows in the water when exposed to ultraviolet light.

Dharavi
Once its own island, this is now India's biggest slum, a place of unregulated housing and artisanal creativity!

Ma Hajiani Dargah
Most Sufi shrines honour male saints but this one celebrates a woman who came here from Arabia over 700 years ago.

Nehru Planetarium
One of five Nehru planetariums in India, all named after the country's first prime minister, Jawaharlal Nehru.

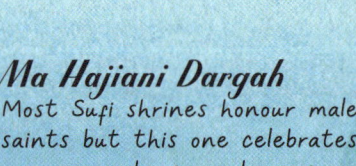

Sea slugs
These brightly coloured marine creatures can be found in Mumbai's waters.

Bombay duck
A battered and fried fish dish.

Nēnē
A close relative of the Canada goose, the nēnē is the state bird of Hawai'i.

Mount Wai'ale'ale
This dormant volcano is one of the wettest spots on Earth.

Waimea Canyon
Known as the Grand Canyon of the Pacific, this canyon stretches 22.5 kilometres.

Hawaiian monk seal
One of the world's most endangered seals, found only in Hawai'i.

Poke
A dish of raw fish, originally a cheap snack made by fisherfolk from leftover catch.

Polynesian Cultural Center
Opened in 1963, this museum showcases the rich cultures of Polynesia.

'Iolani Palace
Built in 1882, this royal residence housed King Kalākaua and Queen Lili'uokalani. In the 1890s, American sugar planters overthrew the government. Hawai'i later became the 50th US state.

Hoary bat
A solitary mammal named for its frosted, silvery coat.

Koa
A precious wood used for making musical instruments like the ukelele.

Pearl Harbour
This naval base became well-known after coming under attack by Japan in 1941, causing the US to join the Second World War.

Hawaiian gardenia
This endemic plant from the coffee family, known as na'u, is critically endangered – just 20 remain in the wild.

Black coral
Soft coral often found at depths of 100 metres.

Humpback whales
These mammals migrate to Hawai'i's warm waters to mate and give birth each year.

HAWAI'I IS THE ONLY US STATE COMPLETELY MADE UP OF ISLANDS. BUT ONLY **SEVEN** OF ITS 132 ISLANDS ARE **INHABITED**.

STATE CAPITAL
HONOLULU

LANGUAGES
ENGLISH, HAWAIIAN, HAWAIIAN CREOLE (PIDGIN)

POPULATION
~1.4 MILLION

Around 1,500 years ago, **voyagers** from the Polynesian islands of Marquesas reached Hawai'i, followed by Tahitians 500 years later. In the 1700s, a British explorer named Captain Cook 'discovered' the islands for the West and introduced diseases that caused the deaths of many Indigenous people.

HAWAI'I
USA
ISLANDS BORN FROM FIRE

Far out in the Pacific Ocean, over 3,800 kilometres from the nearest continent, lies Hawai'i — a string of islands born from fire.

Millions of years ago, volcanoes erupted beneath the ocean, creating new land that rose above the waves. These volcanic forces still shape the Big Island of Hawai'i today.

Hawai'i's lush green valleys, towering mountains and sandy beaches feel like paradise, yet the islands are powerful reminders of nature's forces. The first people to arrive here believed every part of nature had a spirit – the waves that crash on the shore, the rainfall that feeds the forests, and the fiery volcanoes themselves.

At the heart of these beliefs is Pele, a fire goddess said to dwell in Kīlauea, one of the world's most active volcanoes. Many Hawaiians still honour Pele and treat the land, or 'āina, with respect, knowing these islands are alive with stories of creation.

Hawaiian guitar
This lap instrument is played by sliding a steel bar across the strings instead of pressing the frets with your fingers.

'Ōhi'a lehua
A sacred tree associated with Pele, the volcano goddess. Incredibly, it can grow where lava flows.

Kukui
This candlenut tree provides oil from its nuts and wood for canoe building.

The island's highest point.

Mauna Loa
The largest active volcano in the world.

Mauna Kea

Surfing
Hawai'i is the birthplace of modern surfing. Waves here can reach heights of over 9 metres!

Starfruit
Introduced to Hawai'i by Chinese sandalwood traders, this tropical fruit is more commonly grown in gardens than on farms.

'Akaka Falls
A 135-metre tall waterfall.

'Elepaio
A small flycatcher indigenous to the islands' forests.

Ma'ohauhele
The native yellow hibiscus is the official state flower of Hawai'i.

BIG ISLAND

Hawaiian stilt bird
A black-and-white shorebird with long pink legs and a distinctive 'kip-kip-kip' call.

Hula
A dance by women that tells the stories and places of the islands, accompanied by songs or chants called mele.

ISLA MUJERES

MEXICO
WOMEN ISLAND

Where the calm waters of the Gulf of Mexico meet the wild waves of the Caribbean Sea, a small island rises from the blue. This is Isla Mujeres – 'Women Island'.

Bathed in sunshine and surrounded by colourful coral reefs, it has been a place of mystery and legend for centuries. Long ago, the Maya people worshipped Ixchel, the goddess of the Moon, childbirth and medicine. Young girls travelled to the island to leave statues and gifts at her sacred temple, hoping for her blessings as they grew to become women. When Spanish conquerors arrived in the 1500s, they were so taken aback by the many goddess figurines they found there, that they named it 'women island'.

Later, Isla Mujeres became a hideout for pirates and a stopping point for ships crossing the Atlantic during the turmoil of the transatlantic slave trade. Today, it is a peaceful island of fisherfolk, travellers and those who wake early to be the first in Mexico to greet the rising sun.

Whale sharks
Every summer, the world's biggest fish come here to feed on plankton in one of the largest gatherings on Earth.

Tropical storms
Hurricane season runs from June to November, with September and October being the windiest months.

El Meco
A mainland Mayan archaeological site located opposite the island, with a temple dedicated to the rain god Chaac.

ISLA MUJERES LIES ABOUT 13 KILOMETRES OFF THE EASTERN COAST OF THE **YUCATÁN PENINSULA**. UNLIKE MANY LARGER ISLANDS, IT HAS NO OFFICIAL CAPITAL.

LANGUAGES
CH'OL, MAYAN, SPANISH, TZELTAL AND MANY OTHER LANGUAGES AND DIALECTS INDIGENOUS TO MEXICO

POPULATION
~22,000

YONAGUNI

JAPAN
THE ISLAND OF MYSTERIES

Yonaguni is a small, rugged island full of mysteries. As the westernmost island of the Ryukyu Islands, Yonaguni lies at the edge of Japan and is the last place in the country to see the sun set. The weather is warm and tropical, with mild winters and hot summers.

Ryukyu green pigeon
Japan's only endemic pigeon species, native to the island.

Black-banded sea krait
A venomous sea snake which comes to the surface for air every six hours.

Kajiki
Marlin is highly prized for eating. It has pink flesh and is said to be so lean because the fish swim so fast!

Sata andagi
Local doughnuts are flavoured with kokuto, a brown sugar sourced from Okinawa.

Shima tofu
Served cold with shima pakuchii, 'island coriander'.

Chomeiso
A plant in the parsley family which grows wild in Okinawa, used to treat coughs, colds and fevers.

Ryukyu Atlas moth
Has a wingspan of up to 27 centimetres.

Awamori
A rice drink unique to Okinawa and drunk by adults in Yonaguni.

Cape Irizaki
This stone monument marks the westernmost point of Japan, a popular place to watch the sun set.

Sanshin
This snakeskin-covered lute is used in Okinawan music.

Sea grapes
Locally called umibudo, this algae is harvested from island waters and pops in the mouth when eaten.

YONAGUNI ISLAND IS JAPAN'S **WESTERNMOST INHABITED ISLAND**, AND LIES ABOUT 100 KILOMETRES OFF ITS SOUTHERN COAST. IT IS PART OF THE LARGER YAEYAMA VILLAGE WITHIN OKINAWA DISTRICT.

LANGUAGES
JAPANESE, YONAGUNI (ALSO KNOWN AS DUNAN MUNUI)

POPULATION
~1,700

Toyama Ugan
Islanders hold a masked dance at this shrine every year during the Harvest festival in honour of Miruku.

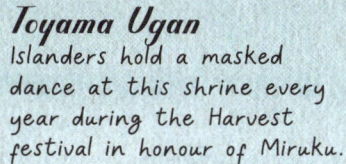

Urano Tombs
Okinawan culture encourages respect for ancestors, as seen in visits to this cemetery that overlooks the sea.

Yonaguni was once part of the Ryūkyū Kingdom, and it has its own language, special weaving traditions, and even a unique breed of horse. Beneath the sea lies the Yonaguni Monument, a mysterious underwater site where huge stone formations look like ancient steps or pyramids. Some believe they are the remains of a lost city.

The island's history is full of mystery, too. Legend says that, in the 1400s, Yonaguni was ruled by a woman named Sanai Isoba. She is said to have been a great leader, and people still celebrate her every year with special ceremonies. Even older legends say that a goddess (or god) named Miruku once wanted to rule the island, but was tricked in a flower contest by a god named Saku (folk versions of the Maitreya and Shakyamuni Buddhas). After Miruku left, the island started to lose its happiness and good harvests. Islanders still hold a Harvest Festival to lure Miruku back.

Thindabana
Said to be the birthplace of the legendary female warrior Sanai Isoba.

SONAI

Goya chanpuru
This bitter melon is a local summer vegetable.

Rokujo Beach
A tiny beach with steep cliffs and a coral garden.

Higashizaki lighthouse
It's 97 steps to the top of this lighthouse with panoramic views.

Yonaguni horse
Native to the island, these small packhorses once carried rice and sugarcane.

Japanese night heron
Now a threatened species, this small brown bird breeds in Japan from May to July.

Hammerhead sharks
Experienced divers venture into 'shivers' of these fish, which swim in female groups.

Yonaguniori
This special weaving technique uses threads dyed with local plants and soil to create kimono fabric.

Tachigami Rock
A natural sea stack where people stop and take romantic selfies!

Ninjin shirishiri
A local dish made with carrots and egg, served for lunch in bento boxes.

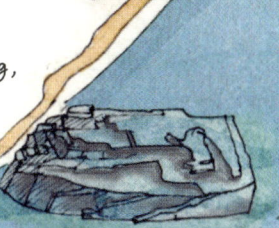

Yuna
Planted on the coast as a barrier against tsunamis... and used to make toilet paper!

Yonaguni Monument
This mysterious underwater rock formation was only discovered by divers in 1987.

Yonaguni's waters are a popular spot for **divers**, especially in winter (December–April) when large schools of hammerhead sharks visit. It's one of the few places in Japan where you can see these magnificent creatures up close.

MOUNT PUTUO
CHINA
THE ISLAND OF COMPASSION

Far out in the sea, off China's eastern coast, lies a peaceful island called Mount Putuo. It is one of the four sacred mountains of Chinese Buddhism and has been a place of prayer for over a thousand years. Pilgrims travel from across the world to honour Guanyin, the goddess of kindness and compassion, hoping she will hear their wishes.

More than thirty temples stand on the island, their stone walls carved with dragons and sacred words. An ancient inscription praises Guanyin's compassion, describing it as 'the voice of the sea's tide, magnificent, rich and harmonious'. While Guanyin was originally depicted as male in India, where Buddhism originated, she evolved into a gender-neutral figure in East Asia, before eventually being worshipped as a goddess here. Women often ask her for help with pregnancy.

The island's warm, misty air carries the scent of the ocean, and gentle sea breezes rustle through its forests. From the highest peaks, visitors are treated to sweeping views of the sea, making them feel as if they are standing between heaven and earth.

EAST CHINA SEA

Fish maw
A fishy dish made by stewing the dried swim bladder of large fish, such as sturgeon.

Guanyin's cave
This small grotto contains rock carvings of the goddess Guanyin, along with porcelain statues draped in cloth.

Longjing prawns
Prawns cooked with pan-roasted tea leaves from Zhejiang Province.

Grass jelly
Served cold in cubes, this dessert is often paired with coloured kidney beans, tapioca and fresh fruit.

Large yellow croaker
This saffron-coloured fish is now protected due to overfishing.

Buddha's tea
Putuo Fo Cha is a green tea made from leaves harvested on the island for over 2,500 years.

Carpinus putoensis
The world's only surviving specimen of this small tree species is found on Putuo Shan.

Wan Fo Pagoda
'Wan Fo' translates to 'Ten Thousand Buddhas' – referring to the 10,000 Buddha statues found inside.

Ginkgo biloba
A large tree with delicate leaves – it can live for up to 1,000 years.

Wandao waxberry
A sweet red tree berry native to Zhoushan, used to treat diseases since ancient times.

Razor clams
A popular seafood delicacy, harvested from the sand.

Huiji Temple
A Buddhist temple located at the island's highest point, Buddha's Summit Peak (291 metres).

Folding Mountain
The island's highest point, Buddha's Summit Peak, can be reached in under an hour by foot or quicker still via cable car.

Mount Putuo is a short boat ride from Shanghai, one of the world's largest cities and busiest ports. Both sit in the **Yangtze River Delta**, where the fertile waters, enriched by silt, remain abundant with fish.

Neolitsea sericea
The golden-haired tree, endangered in China.

Fayu Temple
Nestled among camphor trees, the temple boasts seven worship halls and a Chinese dragon on its roof.

Guanyin's Leap
This cliff bears a footprint, believed to be Guanyin's, from when she leapt over to nearby Luojia Shan Island.

Duobao Pagoda
Also known as the 'Many Treasures Pagoda', it contains statues of the Buddha in various forms.

Buddhism Museum
A small museum filled with relics from the Ming and Qing dynasties.

Bukengu Guanyin Hall
The island's oldest temple, built after a Japanese monk found himself unable to leave Putuo Shan, believing Guanyin's winds were holding him back.

Guanyin statue
This 33-metre tall bronze statue of the goddess Guanyin towers over the land.

MOUNT PUTUO IS IN THE **ZHOUSHAN ARCHIPELAGO**, LOCATED OFF CHINA'S EASTERN COAST IN THE EAST CHINA SEA. IT SITS ABOUT 160 KILOMETRES OFF SHANGHAI.

CAPITAL
DINGHAI (ARCHIPELAGO ZHOUSHAN)

LANGUAGES
MANDARIN, WU CHINESE AND OTHER REGIONAL DIALECTS

POPULATION
~7,471

PILGRIMAGE
19TH DAY OF THE 2ND, 6TH AND 9TH LUNAR MONTH OF THE CHINESE CALENDAR

Fin whales
These baleen whales swim into Sicilian waters in February and March to feed.

Sicilian saint festivals
Sicilians celebrate patron saints with lively festivals – Rosalia in Palermo, Agata in Catania and Lucia in Syracuse.

Granita con brioche
A brioche bun filled with granita – a frozen, sweet treat made from water, sugar and fruit.

Sfinciuni
Sicily's street pizza may have been adapted from ancient Greek flat bread.

Palermo

Cannoli
A pastry filled with different flavours of sweetened, nutty and lemony ricotta cheese.

Bosco della Ficuzza
A large, protected forest, one of three in Sicily.

Gambero rossi
Giant red prawns caught from the island's west coast.

Valley of the Temples
A huge archaeological site built around the fifth century BCE.

SICILY
ITALY
BURSTING WITH FLAVOUR

Nudged by the toe of Italy's 'boot', and lying between Europe and North Africa, Sicily has long been a meeting place of cultures. Over thousands of years, Phoenicians, Greeks, Romans, Arabs, Normans, Spaniards and Bourbons all left their mark, as traders, rulers and immigrants, shaping the island's traditions, architecture and food.

With its rich volcanic soil and warm Mediterranean sun, Sicily bursts with flavour. Golden lemons, sweet oranges and earthy pistachios thrive here, while Sicilian dishes blend spices and culinary techniques from lands near and far.

At the heart of the island's identity is the triskelion – a symbol of strength and good luck. It shows a woman's face surrounded by three running legs – thought to represent the three-pointed island itself. Inspired by the Greek goddess Medusa, it speaks of resilience and defiance, transformation and artistic power – fitting for an island that has been shaped by so many.

Caponata
A sweet-sour stew of aubergines, tomatoes, capers and olives.

Isole Eolie
A group of seven volcanic islands off the northeast coast of Sicily. They are named after Aeolus, keeper of the world's winds.

Pistachio tree
Originally from ancient Persia, this tree-nut was brought here by the Arabs in the ninth century.

The Nebrodi
Mountain range along Sicily's north coast, with forests of cork, beech and oak trees.

Hundred-horse chestnut tree
Tree named after a legend where Queen Joan of Aragon and her 100 knights took shelter beneath its branches during a storm.

Lemons
Those grown on Mount Etna's slopes are especially prized for their unique tangy flavour.

Sicilian wolf
A now-extinct subspecies of wolf that was endemic to Sicily.

Mount Etna
This volcano has been active for over 2 million years.

Towering over the island, **Mount Etna** is Europe's tallest and most active volcano. Its eruptions have shaped the island's landscapes for millennia, creating rich soil for farmland. Etna's fiery presence is woven into Sicily's history, mythology and daily life.

Thapsos
A prehistoric village where Middle Bronze Age civilization thrived.

Val di Noto
A group of marble-encrusted towns, rebuilt in the Baroque style in the seventeenth century after an earthquake.

Archimedes
The mathematician, astronomer and inventor was born in Syracuse in 287 BCE.

Graeco-Roman theatre
The largest ancient Greek theatre in Sicily, later used by the Romans.

Arancini
These breaded, deep-fried rice balls are believed to have entered Sicilian cuisine during Arab rule.

SICILY IS THE LARGEST ISLAND IN THE **MEDITERRANEAN SEA**. IT SITS JUST OFF THE SOUTHERN COAST OF ITALY.

CAPITAL
PALERMO

LANGUAGES
ARABIC, ITALIAN, SICILIAN

POPULATION
~5 MILLION

N — MEDITERRANEAN SEA

LESVOS

GREECE

AN ISLAND OF POETRY AND LOVE

Lesvos is a large Greek island in the Aegean Sea, just across from Türkiye. With its warm summers and mild winters, the island enjoys a Mediterranean climate in which the abundant olive trees thrive.

The island has a long and rich history. It played an important role in ancient Greece, and was mentioned in the poet Homer's *Iliad* as an island of women skilled in handicrafts. Through the centuries, Lesvos was ruled by the Byzantine and Ottoman Empires, before becoming part of Greece again in 1912.

But more than its battles and rulers, Lesvos is famous for being the birthplace of Sappho, the poet and musician who transformed Greek literature. Nearly 3,000 years ago, Sappho published short, intimate poems about her life, at a time when female voices were rarely heard outside the home and most literature was about epic battles and male heroes. Today, the legacy of ancient poetry still lingers.

With one of the shortest sea crossings into Europe from outside, the island is a place of refuge for those fleeing war and hardship.

Molyvos Castle — Built by the Byzantines, this medieval fortress still overlooks the harbour today.

Orpheus's song — In Greek mythology, the hero Orpheus's still-singing head and lyre washed ashore here.

Kaimaki — This sticky ice cream is flavoured with tree resin gathered from neighbouring Chios.

Petrified Forest — Volcanic eruptions 20 million years ago preserved cinnamon and other trees.

Eressos Acropolis — Ancient settlement which stands on the hill, said to be the birthplace of the poet Sappho.

Krüper's nuthatch — A tiny but vocal bird, its song is rapid, loud and high-pitched.

Sigri Castle — This Ottoman fort once protected the island from pirates!

Kalloni sardines — Local sardines prized for their taste, as well as for being sustainably fished.

Rock of Skala Eressos — A popular spot where daredevils swim out to climb and jump off the rock.

Olives — Olives are the island's biggest export, and Lesvos is famous for its olive oil.

Seal caves — Mediterranean monk seals use caves along the island's coastline to breed.

VIS
CROATIA
A BUSTLING TRADE HUB WORTHY OF A PIRATE QUEEN

Vis, surrounded by the calm blue waters of the Adriatic Sea, has been a bustling trade hub for centuries. Located off the coast of Croatia, this small island was a popular stop for sailors thanks to its freshwater and strategic position.

Long ago, Queen Teuta of the Aridiaei tribe in Illyria made Vis the centre of rebellion against the domineering Roman empire. In the third century BCE, she defied the Romans by encouraging piracy against their ships. Over time, the island saw a dizzying number of different rulers, from the ancient Greeks to the Romans, Venetians and Austrians.

During the Second World War, Vis became the headquarters of the Yugoslav Partisans under Josip Broz Tito, who then ruled Yugoslavia (which included Croatia) for 35 years. Until the breakup of Yugoslavia in 1991 and Croatian independence, the island was used as a military base, closed off to outsiders. This isolation helped Vis retain its rich biodiversity, which includes 126 bird species, along with many rare bats and lizards.

N — ADRIATIC SEA

European bee-eater
These sociable birds nest, feed and roost communally.

Queen's Cave
Said to be Queen Teuta's home, it consists of five interconnected caverns.

Komiža
The island's harbour and medieval fishing village.

Peka
A lamb, veal or seafood dish cooked over an open fire.

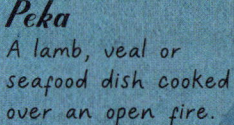

Modra Špilja
Located just 5 kilometres southwest of Vis, this cave fills with blue light every morning.

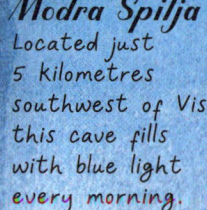

Eleonora's falcon
About 100 pairs nest here. Named after Eleanor of Sardinia, who protected the birds by law in 1392.

Cuttlefish risotto
This savoury rice dish, dyed black with cuttlefish ink, is a legacy of Venetian rule from the fifteenth to eighteenth centuries.

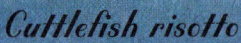

Pršut
Smoky Dalmatian ham, air-dried and salted by the fierce Bura wind from the Adriatic.

Scilly bees
Rare orange-brown insects, free from some of the diseases affecting bees on mainland Britain.

Spotted cowrie
Shells found on the white sands of Rushy Bay.

King Charles's Castle
A fort built during Tudor times and occupied by Royalists during the Civil War.

Iron Age warrior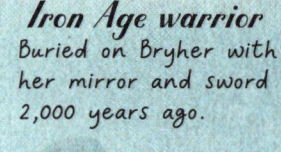
Buried on Bryher with her mirror and sword 2,000 years ago.

BRYHER

SCILLY

ENGLAND

ISLES OF SHIPWRECKS AND SUNSHINE

Travel back to Scilly during the Stone Age and you will discover one single landmass, dotted with settlements: 'Ennor', the great island, as it's known in its Cornish tongue. Zoom forward to the present, and the sea has risen over fields and pathways, creating an archipelago of islands skittering out into the Celtic Sea. These are the Isles of Scilly.

People have lived in Scilly for thousands of years, farming the land and fishing. Due to high winds and winter gales, there have been more shipwrecks around these shores than anywhere else in the world. The islands were fortified during Elizabeth I's reign after the Spanish Armada planned to use them during their attack, and later became a royal base during the English Civil Wars.

Today, every island in the archipelago has its own independent spirit. Palm trees sway in gentle breezes on balmy Tresco Island, while St Agnes often claims to be the first place in Britain to greet the spring in February. At the lowest tides, the sea reveals lost paths, letting you walk between islands, just as people did long ago in the days of Ennor.

Speckled wood
This butterfly is found widely on the islands during the warmer months.

SAMSON
Once home to a small community that was cleared in the nineteenth century. Visitors can now wander through the hilltop houses.

Scilly shrew
A native rodent which lives by the beach and eats sandhoppers.

ST AGNES

N

ATLANTIC OCEAN

Troytown ice cream
Farmed by the same family since the Civil War, the rich milk from their Jersey cows is now used to make delicious ice cream.

TEXEL

THE NETHERLANDS

WHERE TULIPS SPRING FROM ANCIENT SOIL

A long time ago, powerful forces shaped Texel. During the Ice Age, giant glaciers carried clay all the way from Scandinavia, leaving behind rich soil that still covers the island today.

Later, in 1170, a giant flood swept through the land, separating Texel from the mainland and making it the southernmost of the Frisian Islands - a chain of sandy isles stretching along the coast of the Netherlands and Germany.

Because of its mild climate, sea air and sandy-clay soil, Texel is an ideal place to grow flower bulbs such as tulips. In recent years there's been a shift towards more sustainable farming practices, and on Texel the sea winds help keep pests away, meaning that fewer pesticides are needed. Every spring, the island's fields burst into a rainbow of red, yellow, purple and pink. Poppies, daffodils, hyacinths and snowdrops join the show, painting the island in blooms which colour the day.

But as the sun sets, another kind of show begins. Because of its low levels of light pollution, Texel's dark skies twinkle with stars, making it a lovely place to gaze at the universe above.

NORTH SEA

Peregrine falcons
These birds of prey can fly at speeds twice as fast as most cars.

Nightingale
This iconic endangered songbird migrates between Africa and Europe, occasionally stopping at Texel during its journey.

Saline vegetables
Delicious plants grow near or in the sea, such as marsh samphire and seaweed.

Texelstroom
This ferry is more eco-friendly than most, running on compressed natural gas, electricity and solar power as well as diesel.

Texel is a paradise for **birds**! Over 400 species stop here to rest during migration. From elegant spoonbills to swooping peregrine falcons, the island is alive with the sounds of flapping wings and birdsong.

Great auk
Britain's last flightless bird became extinct after the last one was killed in Papa Westray in 1813.

NORTH RONALDSAY

Seaweed-eating sheep
North Ronaldsay is home to an ancient breed of sheep that only eat seaweed.

Northern lights
The aurora borealis, known locally as the 'Merry Dancers', lights up the night sky.

White-tailed sea eagles
These birds of prey thrive in Orkney after a successful reintroduction as a protected species.

SANDAY

STRONSAY

Start Point Lighthouse
First lit in 1806, this was the first lighthouse in Scotland with a revolving light.

Light in the North
Built by Norse rulers in 1137, St Magnus's Cathedral still dominates the Orkney landscape.

Seaweed
Long used as a fertilizer and food, seaweed was also collected centuries ago to produce a substance for use in soap and glassmaking.

The Westray Wife
A farmhouse cheese named after a very rare tiny Neolithic figurine found on the same island.

ORKNEY
SCOTLAND
AN ISLAND SET IN STONE

Off Scotland's northern coast, where rugged land meets a restless sea, lie the islands of Orkney — a place where the past whispers through the wind. Ancient art and engineering sit on soft green hills, while salt-laced air carries tales as old as time.

Thousands of years ago, Stone Age (or Neolithic) people called these islands home. They built mighty stone monuments — circles and tombs that still stand today. Some were gathering places, others used as calendars, or sacred sites to give thanks to the sun for crops and new birth. No one knows for sure why the communities came together to build such imposing sites. But it seems that they were celebrating the mysterious, powerful connection between humans and the world around them. Even now, cattle graze where their ancestors' once did, in a tradition stretching back to the Stone Age.

Later, Vikings arrived, drawn by Orkney's rich soil and wild seas. Though the islands became part of Scotland in the 1400s, they kept their own spirit — one woven from ancient stones, Norse mythology and folklore of Selkies and Trows.

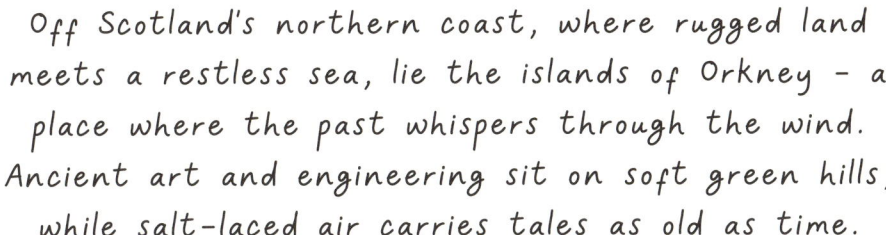

BAFFIN
CANADA
THE ARCTIC WILDLIFE HIGHWAY

Far in the icy north, where Canada meets the Arctic, lies the fifth-largest island in the world: Qikiqtaaluk, as the Inuit people called it, or Baffin Island, as it was later named by Europeans, after the British explorer who mapped it. Shaped by nature, it's a land of jagged peaks, glacier-carved valleys and breathtaking fjords.

Each spring, as the sun climbs higher, Baffin Island wakes from its deep winter sleep. Frozen fjords crack and melt, creating a remarkable 'wildlife highway'. Seals, polar bears and narwhals, often dubbed 'the unicorns of the sea', all gather here - with some remaining ever-present all year round.

Hunting and trapping is a way of life for the Inuit, who have inhabited this island for centuries and are still deeply connected to the land and sea. Wild and untamed, this is an island where nature reigns and Arctic wilderness thrives.

Baffin is home to several **Inuit communities** who blend cultural practices such as hunting, trapping and fishing with modern technology. They work to preserve their language, art and stories while adapting to their changing environment, and to reclaim names, practices and spiritual connections to the land, many of which were altered by **colonialism**.

Polar bears
These mammals are 'pagophilic', meaning they love ice. Their existence is threatened by melting polar ice caps.

Snowy owl
A master of camouflage, this large white owl hunts lemmings and other small prey.

Arctic berries
Edible berries, leaves and roots are used raw, in tea or in Inuit ice cream.

Arctic woolly bear moth
This moth's caterpillar life cycle lasts around seven years.

Narwhal's tusk
Recently discovered to be a sensory organ. Inuit people also used tusks for tools, from tent poles to fishing gear.

Sedna
Inuit sea goddess, mother of all sea creatures.

Palaugaaq
A fried bread, also known as bannock, introduced by Europeans.

ARCTIC OCEAN

ONCE UPON MY ISLAND HOME

In creating this book, I spoke with women from each island who kindly shared stories of their island home and what it means to them.

'Women tend to work in the fields in CHILOÉ, but we are proud to be working at sea.'

MIRIAM VIDAL MILLACURA
Huilliche representative of the National Network of Fisherwomen

'I am a strong culture woman who fights to protect the traditions of the TIWI people.'

CAROL PURUNTATAMERI
Artist and Tiwi elder

'WAIHEKE'S 'Marae' sits in tikanga. It is steeped in Māori history... It nurtures every aspect of my wellbeing.'

MAIKARA ROPATA
A wisdom keeper and grandmother in Te Ao Māori

'From the very beginning, THE SEYCHELLES was a melting pot of three continents.'

BERNADETTE WILLEMIN
Director General of Marketing for Tourism

'MADAGASCAR influences how I paint. I show mainly Brown and Black people. Representation is vital.'

SAWYER CLOUD
Illustrator

'Preserving the AMAZON for the entire world is incredibly important.'

PEDRINA BRITO DE MENDONÇA
Leader of the Saracá Community, Brazil

'On the Uros Islands in LAKE TITICACA, we carry our grandparents' communal wisdom. Despite scarcity, we have hope.'

DINA DÍAZ
Headmistress of School 70682, Uros Islands

'These seven islands of MUMBAI reflect all the beautiful diversity of India. No wonder it is such a creative place.'

TARAN KHAN
Author

'We love to have fun and spread sunshine in SAMOA. Family bonds mean that we are really happy.'

BRIANNA FRUEAN
Activist and environmental advocate for Samoa

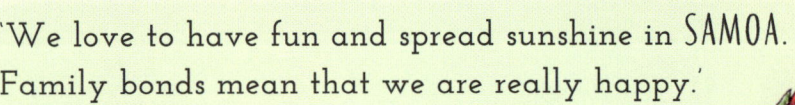

'Many of our songs and dances in HAWAI'I are in honour of the goddess Pele.'

KANANI OLIVEIRA
Hula practitioner

'ISLA MUJERES is a very rewarding place to teach. My daughter will be the first in our family to graduate.'

MAYRA YOLANDA (YOLI) TEC CHUNAB
Teacher of children of migrants

'In YONAGUNI you are two minutes from the sea, three minutes from the mountains.'

MARISA FUKUMINE
Town Hall chronicler of the island's history

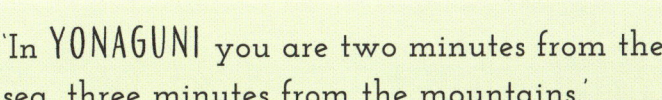

'When you've been friends with MOUNT PUTUO and the sea as long as I have, they become a part of you.'

AUNTIE HONG
Restaurant and guesthouse owner

'From every clash, an encounter is born; in SICILY, where worlds collide, new stories emerge.'

ROSA LOMBARDO
Watercolour artist

'We are farming in the old style in LESVOS but with a new philosophy.'

MARIA VALILI
Organic farmer

'Every house in VIS has a little garden with olive trees.'

MARINA VOJKOVIĆ
Runs Planet Vis, an island travel company

'SCILLY astounds me daily with its natural beauty.'

RACHEL LEWIN
Headteacher

'I love the calmness of TEXEL, where the gentle breeze sweeps over fields of vibrant tulips.'

KLAARTJE REUVERS
Flower bulb grower

'There is a great sense of island identity in each of the ORKNEY islands.'

JOCELYN RENDALL
Farmer and writer

'In BAFFIN, we understand that connection to the Earth isn't a belief, it's a reality. You are an animal, I am an animal.'

AIJA KOMANGAPIK
Seal hunter, artist and Seal Products Manager for Isaruit Inuit Arts

BEYOND THE ISLAND

Island communities face similar challenges, shaped by history, geography and climate. Though separated by oceans, their stories often overlap — from ancient and recent histories of colonization and forced labour to today's fight for identity, land and survival in a warming world. These questions help unpack some of the histories and issues explored in this book.

WHY DO THE NAMES OF SOME ISLANDS AND PLACES CHANGE OVER TIME?

Island names reflect layers of **history, culture** and **power**. Some are indigenous, others imposed by **outsiders, colonizers** or different **empires** over time. Some are a mixture. Here are a few examples:

- **Texel** (from the ancient Germanic for 'southern')
- **Lesvos** (ΛΈΣΒΟΣ in Greek, meaning 'forested', an endonym)
- **Vis** (Croatian version of the ancient Greek Issa)
- **Putuo** (Chinese form of Sanskrit Potalaka from India)
- **Baffin Island** (British colonial name. The Inuit name, Qikiqtaaluk, means 'big island')
- **Isla Mujeres** (Spanish name; the original Mayan name is lost)
- **Orkney** (colonial Norse name, Orkneyjar, may be a version of an older native name)
- **Sicily** (English version of the Italian Sicilia)
- **Yonaguni** (name given to the island by people from a different part of Japan: an exonym)
- **Seychelles** (named after an eighteenth-century French politician)

Today, many places are restoring original names to **honour local cultures** and **reclaim identity**, like Mumbai, renamed after the fisherfolk goddess Mumba.

WHY WERE ISLANDS SO OFTEN COLONIZED BY FARAWAY COUNTRIES?

Some of the European islands in this book were colonized many times in their early history. From the fifteenth century, European powers began expanding overseas, claiming islands along sea routes to secure resources and trade and establish military bases. Islands like Mumbai, Isla Mujeres and Waiheke were seized without local consent. Over time, many islanders fought for their independence. Some were absorbed into new post-colonial nations. Some, like Hawai'i, remain territories or distant states, reflecting lingering colonial ties.

WHAT WAS THE TRANSATLANTIC SLAVE TRADE, AND HOW DOES IT CONNECT TO THE ISLANDS?

Between the 1500s and 1800s, millions of Africans were enslaved and transported across oceans by European and US enslavers to work on plantations. Many islands, including Isla Mujeres, the Seychelles and Madagascar, were plantation economies using enslaved populations. The slave trade deeply shaped island societies, cultures and populations, with its legacy still felt today.

WHAT IS CLIMATE JUSTICE, AND WHY IS IT IMPORTANT FOR ISLANDS?

Climate justice means acknowledging that those least responsible for climate change often suffer its harshest effects. Island nations, like Samoa, contribute little to global emissions but face devastating environmental impacts. Climate justice calls for fair action – financial aid, protection of land, and ensuring island communities have a strong voice in global decisions.

WHY IS IT IMPORTANT TO TALK TO PEOPLE FROM THE ISLANDS TO GAIN FIRSTHAND EXPERIENCE?

Local people, wherever they are in the world, have knowledge which books, maps and the internet may not reflect. Their voices, histories and stories offer vital firsthand perspectives on their past, present and future. Listening to them ensures that their realities are understood, respected and prioritized in any conversations about island life.

GLOSSARY

Aboriginal Means 'original inhabitant' in Latin, and when used with a capital A, it refers to the Indigenous peoples of Australia.

Ancestral Something passed down from earlier members of your family.

Artisanal A product that has been made in a traditional way by a skilled creator.

Baleen Found in some whales' mouths instead of teeth, they are used to filter krill out of the water.

Biodiversity The kinds of plants and animals in an area, and how many of them there are.

Colonialism A system where one country, the colonizer, has control over another country.

Coniferous A tree that keeps its leaves all year round.

Coralline Resembling or related to coral.

Endangered A species that is close to becoming extinct (no longer in existence).

Endemic A species that is only found in one particular place.

Endonym The name used by people who live in that place.

Empire When a group of countries are ruled by people from a completely different place.

Exonym A name used for a place by people from outside it.

Extinct Something which no longer exists, such as an animal, plant or language.

Fauna The animals of a place.

Fjord A long, narrow strip of sea surrounded on three sides by steep rocks or cliffs, formed by glaciers.

Flora The plants that grow in an area.

Immigrant Someone who has moved from their home country to live in another country.

Indigenous The first people to live in a place, before others came and took over the land (often called colonization). Some Indigenous people say it's important to remember that everyone comes from somewhere, and that people who moved to the land later – like settlers – should also be called by where they came from, such as 'European' or 'settler'.

Macropod A type of marsupial – an animal where the young is carried in a pouch after they're born, such as a kangaroo or wallaby.

Matrilineal A system where your ancestors are traced back through women – the maternal line.

Micronation A group that has claimed independence, but this independence is not recognized by everyone.

Microstate A country with both a very small population and area.

Migrate To temporarily travel to a new place to live.

Native Someone who was born in a particular country, or a plant or animal that grows or lives naturally in a place.

Nomadic A way of living where people migrate (often with the seasons, from one place and back again) rather than staying put all year round.

Non-binary A gender that is neither exclusively male nor female.

Patrilineal A system where your ancestors are traced back through men – the paternal line.

Rite Usually part of a ceremony, following a specific process, with set words and actions.

Ritual A ceremony or practice where the same thing is done every time.

Royalist Someone who believes that a king or queen should rule over a country.

Sacred Something that is holy.

Selkie A mythical creature that looks like a seal in water and sheds its skin to walk on land as a human.

Settler Member of a population which arrived from elsewhere and took over a land from its Indigenous people.

Sovereign republic An independent state where the people who live there have the power to elect officials.

Trow An Orcadian version of Scandinavia's mischievous trolls.

Verdant An area covered in green plants.

INDEX

Animals
Amazon river dolphin – 29
Arctic fox – 53
Arctic Woolly Bear Moth – 52
Aye-aye – 19
Baffin Island wolf – 53
Bare-throated tiger heron – 35
Barren-ground caribou – 53
Beluga whale – 53
Black banded sea krait – 36
Black coral – 32
Blue whale – 15
Bolivian vizcacha – 20
Brush-tailed rabbit-rats – 25
Bryde's whale – 17
Bush stone-curlew – 25
Butterflies – 18
Chilean dolphin – 14
Coconut crab – 23
Coelacanth – 18
Coral – 27, 35
Crested terns – 24
Dairy sheep – 43
Dalmatian wall lizard – 45
Darwin's Fox – 15
Dugongs – 25
Dumeril's boa – 19
Eleonora's falcon – 45
European Bee-Eater – 44
Fin whale – 40
Flamingo – 21, 31
Flat-billed kingfisher – 23
Fossa – 19
Frigatebird – 35
Fruit bats – 27
Gambero rosso – 40
Giant catfish – 29
Giant goby – 47
Giant leaf-tailed gecko – 19
Giant otter – 29
Greenback Firecrown – 15
Hammerhead shark – 37
Hawaiian monk seal – 32
Hawaiian stilt bird – 33
Hawksbill turtle – 27
Hoary bat – 32
Humpback whale – 32
Humboldt penguin – 14
Jaguar – 28
Japanese night heron – 37
Kajiki (marlin) – 36
Kaka – 17
Korora – 16
Krüper's nuthatch – 42
Kuaka – 17
Large yellow croakers – 38
Lemming – 53
Llama – 21
Madagascan plover – 19
Magellanic penguin – 14
Monk seal – 42
Narwhal – 52
Nene – 32
Nightingale – 49
Nile crocodile – 19
Northern brush-tailed phascogale – 25
Olive ridley sea turtle – 25
Oi (grey-faced petrel) – 16
Palythoa mutuki – 30
Peregrine falcon – 49
Polar bear – 52
Puffin – 50
Puna ibis – 20
Pudú – 15
Pygmy blue whales – 18
Rawaru (blue cod fish) – 17
Ryukyu Atlas moth – 36
Ryukyu green pigeon – 36
Saltwater crocodile – 25
Samoan Flying Fox – 23
Sardine – 43
Scilly bee – 46
Scilly shrew – 46
Sea slug – 30
Sea turtle – 35
Seal – 48
Seaweed-eating sheep – 51
Seychelles giant tortoise – 26
Seychelles scops-owl – 26
Seychelles sunbird – 26
Seychelles swiftlets – 27
Seychelles warbler – 27
Sicilian wolf – 41
Snow goose – 53
Snowy owl – 52
Southern river otter – 15
Speckled wood – 46
Spider tortoise – 19
Spoonbill – 48
Texel sheep – 48
Tiger chameleons – 26
Titicaca duck – 20
Titicaca water frog – 20
Tiwi hooded robin – 24
Tiwi masked owl – 25
Tooth-billed pigeon – 22
Trout – 20
Tui – 17
Uakari – 28
Vicuña camelid – 20
Wallabies – 24
Whale shark – 34
White-tailed sea eagle – 51
Yacare – 29
Yonaguni horse – 37

Beaches and Bays
Chowpatty beach – 30
Gera's gulf – 43
Kalloni's gulf – 42
Oneroa beach – 16
Playa norte – 34
Rackwick bay – 50
Rokujo beach – 37
Rushy Bay – 46
Stiniva Cove – 45
Te Matuku Bay – 17

Castles
'Iolani Palace – 32
Fortress of Mytilene – 43
King Charles's Castle – 46
Molyvos castle – 42
Sigri castle – 42
Star Castle – 47
The Rova od Antananarivo – 19

Customs and Cultures Festivals
Virgen de La Candelaria, the – 21
Festivals – 43
Ganesh Chaturthi – 31
Harvest festival – 37
Meierblis, the – 48
Ouwe Sunderklaas – 48

Forests & Parks
A'opo Conservation Area – 22
Agguttinni Territorial Park – 53
Duinen van Texel National Park – 48
Forest de Dennen – 48
National Botanical Garden – 26
O Le Pupu-Pue – 23
Onetangi Forest and Bird Reserve – 17
Parque Nacional do Jaú – 28
Parque Pantauco – 15
Praslin National Park – 27
Qaummaarviit Territorial Park – 53
Rainforests of the Atsinanana, The – 19
Titicaca Nature Reserve – 20
Tresco Abbey Garden – 47
Tsingy de Bemaraha – 19

Sacred spaces (shrines, temples, churches)
Bukenqu Guanyin Hall – 39
Duobao Pagoda – 39
El meco – 34
Fayu temple – 39
Guanyin Yangzhi Nunnery – 38
Huiji Temple – 39
Ixchel's temple – 35
Jama Masjid – 31
Ma Hajiana Dargah – 30
Mount Mary Church – 30
Mumba Devi temple – 31
Nuestra Señora del Rosario – 15
Piritahi Marae – 16
Royal Hill of Ambohimanga – 19
Sanctuary of the three gods – 43
Sitaldevi – 31
St Magnus's Cathedral – 51
Toyama Ugan – 37
Triduana's Chapel and Loch – 50
Valley of the Temples – 40
Wan Fo Pagoda – 39
Yeni mosque – 43

Food and Drink
Açaí berries – 28
Arancini – 41
Arctic berry – 52
Awamori – 36
Bombay duck – 30
Bouyon – 26
Brodet – 44
Buddha tea – 38
Camu-camu – 28
Cannoli – 40
Caponata – 40
Cochinita Pibil – 35
Cornish pasty – 47
Curanto – 14
Cuttlefish risotto – 44
Falooda – 30
Farofa – 28
Fish maw – 38
Frito de ispe – 20
Granita con Brioche – 40
Grass jelly – 38
Kaimaki – 42
Kalloni sardine – 42
Kava – 23
Ladob – 27
Ladotyri Mytillinus – 43
Longjong prawns – 38
Marsh samphire – 49
Ninjin Shirishiri – 37
Palaugaaq – 52
Peka – 44
Poke – 32
Pršut – 44
Razor clam – 39
Sata andagi – 36
Satini reken – 27
Sea grapes – 36
Sfinciuni – 40
Sheep's milk ice cream – 48
Shima tofu – 36
Sonai Goya chanpuru – 37
Sopa de lima – 35
Sopa de quinia – 21
The Westray wife – 51
Tikin-Xic – 35
Troytown ice cream – 46
Turtle eggs – 25
Vada pav – 31
Vary and laoka – 18
Vugava – 45
Waiheke herb spread – 17
Yuwurli – 25

Lighthouses
Eierland Lighthouse – 48
Higashizaki Lighthouse – 37
Start Point Lighthouse – 51
Stončica Lighthouse – 45

Mountains
Aracá – 29
Cordillera del Piuchén – 15
Folding Mountain – 39
Mount Hum – 45
Mount Maunganui – 17
Mount Odin – 53
Mount Olympus – 43
Nebrodi Mountains – 41
Sacred Mountains – 20

Museums
Buddhism museum – 39
Cancún underwater museum – 35
Museo de Achao – 15
Mytilene's Archaeological Museum – 43
Patakijiyali museum – 24
Robert Louis Stevenson Museum – 23
Valhalla Museum – 47

Plants
'Ohi'a Lehua – 33
Arctic poppy – 53
Arctic willow – 53
Baobab tree – 19
Carob – 45
Carpinus Putoensis – 39
Chestnut tree – 41
Chomeiso – 36
Cinnamon tree – 26, 42
Coco de mer – 27
Coco leaf – 21
Ebony – 19
Gilt-edged lichen – 47
Ginkgo Biloba – 39
Glasswort – 48
Hawaiian gardenia – 32
Jellyfish tree – 26
Kauri – 16
Koa – 32
Kukui (candlenut tree) – 33
Latanier palm – 26
Lau'ie (padanus) – 22
Lemon – 41
Ma'ohauhele – 33
Madagascan sandalwood – 18
Mahogany tree – 28
Malagasy rosewood – 19
Mangrove – 35
Nalea – 15
Neolitsea Sericea – 39
Nepenthes pervillei – 26
Nut tree – 28
Olive tree – 42
Paperbark trees – 25
Pistachio tree – 41
Reinhold's orchid – 43
Rubber tree – 28
Scented narcissi – 47
Screw pine – 26
Sea aster – 48
Sea holly – 48
Sea lavender – 48
Seaweed – 49, 51
Starfruit – 33
Teuila – 23
Teuta's Bellflower – 45
Tulip – 48
Wandao waxberry – 39
Yuna – 37

Volcanoes
Mauna Kea – 33
Mauna Loa – 33
Mount Etna – 41
Mount Matavanua – 22
Mount Wai'ale'ale – 32

FURTHER READING

If you enjoyed the island stories in this book, here are some other books to help you explore even more of the world.

Amazing Islands by Sabrina Weiss and Kerry Hyndman
Atlas of Adventures by Lucy Letherland
Islands by Ben Lerwill and Li Zhang
Maps by Aleksandra and Daniel Mizielinski

ACKNOWLEDGEMENTS

The year it took to research and write this book coincided with turmoil across the world. Thank you to all those who nevertheless gave their time to be interviewed or who commented on drafts. It has been a privilege to communicate with you.

Chiloé: Miriam Vidal Millacura, Stephanie Prieto Trincado, Tito and Valentina Infante Willson.
Waiheke: Maikara Ropata, Tanya Butt.
Madagascar: Sawyer Cloud.
Lake Titicaca: Dina Díaz, Carmela and Miguel Coquis, Jessica Luong, Nonato Rufino Chuqimamani Valer.
Samoa: Brianna Fruean.
Tiwi: Carol Puruntatameri, Tandanya Allain.
Seychelles: Bernadette Willemin.
Amazon River Islands: Pedrina Brito de Mendonça, Romar Beling.
Mumbai: Taran Khan, Anshika Misra.
Hawaiʻi: Kanani Oliveira, Nainoa Mau, Mary Varilla Jones.
Isla Mujeres: Mayra Yolanda (Yoli) Tec Chunab, Lean on Me International, Sharifa Rhodes-Pitts.
Yonaguni: Marisa Fukumine, Hiroko Dean.
Mount Putuo: Auntie Hong, Xiaolu Guo, Rachel Wang.
Sicily: Rosa Lombardo, Greta Oggioni, Elena Neri.
Lesvos: Maria Valili, Niki Charalampopulou.
Vis: Marina Vojković, Ivana Ivičić.
Scilly: Rachel Lewin, Piers Lewin.
Texel: Klaartje Reuvers, Rose Trap.
Orkney: Jocelyn Rendall.
Baffin: Jessica Kotierk, Hugh Brody, Dr. Martin Nweeia, Narwhal Tusk Research, and Pamela Peeters, Institute for a Sustainable Planet, under a Fulbright-Hayes Grant.
Thank you to Helen Cann for her beautiful illustrations and to the book's editor, Helen Brown, its publisher Rachel Williams, and literary agent, Rebecca Carter, for their tireless hard work and good cheer. And Tito, south to north; Aphra and Adi, end to beginning.

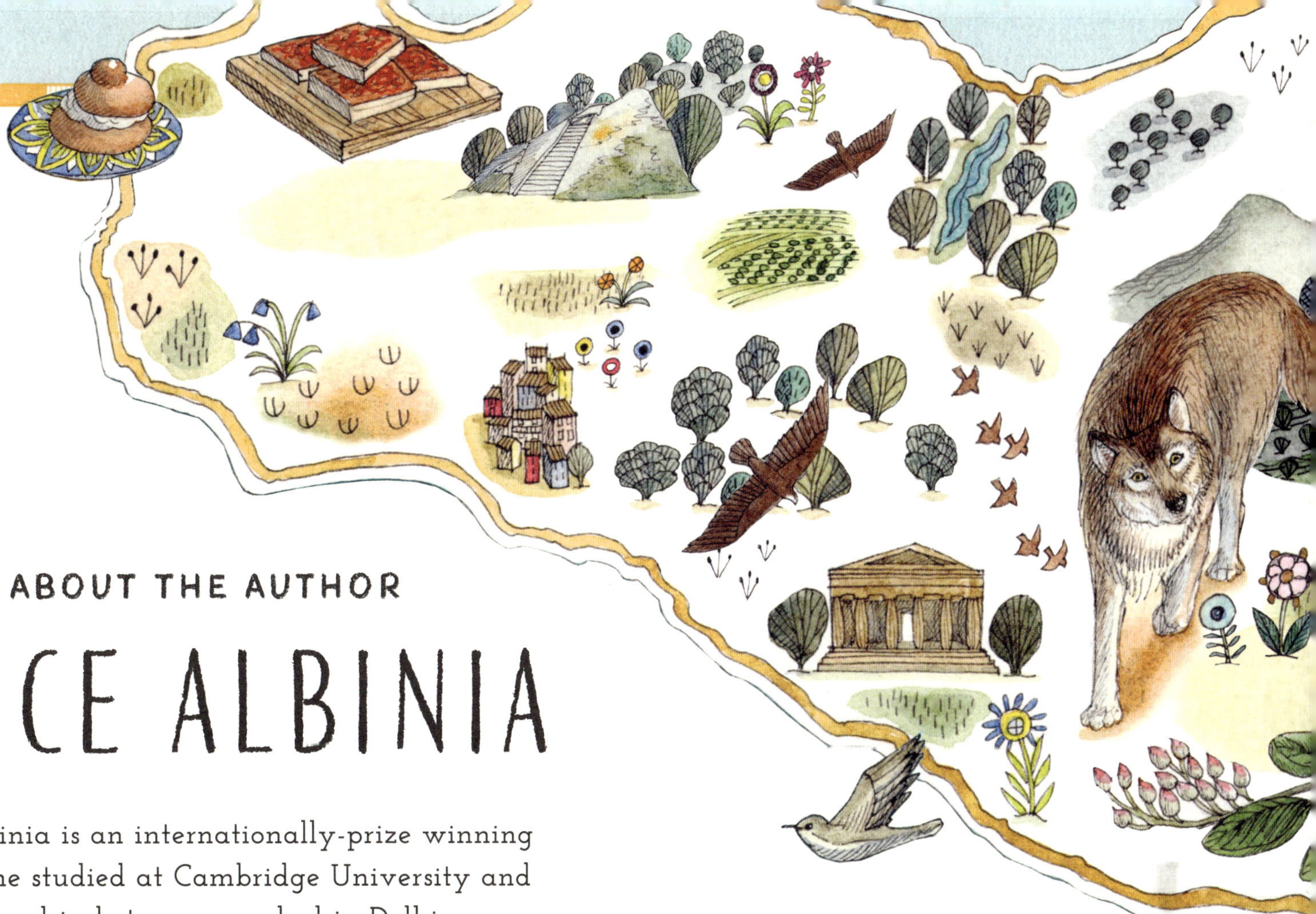

ABOUT THE AUTHOR
ALICE ALBINIA

Alice Albinia is an internationally-prize winning author. She studied at Cambridge University and SOAS, and in between, worked in Delhi as a journalist, editor and critic (years that she looks back on with love and longing). The writing of her first book, *Empires of the Indus: The Story of a River*, took her to Pakistan, India, Afghanistan and beyond.

Alice is renowned for paired fictional and non-fiction books. Both *Empires of the Indus* and her novel *Leela's Book* explore the fates of rivers and the humans that inhabit them. Her later books, the novel *Cwen* and the non-fiction *The Britannias: And the Islands of Women*, written while she was living in Orkney, weave together female mythologies and stories to tell an alternative history of Britain.

Alice is the mother of two daughters, who helped her write this book. *Once Upon an Island* is Alice's debut children's book and was shaped by interviews with women from the islands. She cherished hearing their voices and stories, glimmers of light during a dark time of climate chaos, attacks on Indigenous rights and catastrophe in Palestine.